LEARNING
SUPPORT
SERVICES

Radical Sports
SKATeBOARDiNG

Andy Horsley • • • • • • • • •

Heinemann
LIBRARY

H www.heinemann/library.co.uk
Visit our website to find out more information about Heinemann Library books.

To order:
☎ Phone 44 (0) 1865 888066
▤ Send a fax to 44 (0) 1865 314091
▢ Visit the Heinemann Library Bookshop at www.heinemann/library.co.uk to browse our
catalogue and order online.

First published in Great Britain by Heinemann Library,
Halley Court, Jordan Hill, Oxford OX2 8EJ,
a division of Reed Educational and Professional Publishing Ltd.
Heinemann is a registered trademark of Reed Educational & Professional Publishing Limited.

OXFORD   MELBOURNE   AUCKLAND
JOHANNESBURG   BLANTYRE   GABORONE
IBADAN   PORTSMOUTH NH (USA)   CHICAGO

© Reed Educational and Professional Publishing Ltd 2002
First published in paperback 2003
The moral right of the proprietor has been asserted.

Designed by Celia Floyd
Originated by Universal
Printed in Hong Kong by Wing King Tong

ISBN 0 431 03694 2 (hardback)   ISBN 0 431 03702 7 (paperback)
06 05 04 03   07 06 05 04 03
10 9 8 7 6 5 4 3 2   10 9 8 7 6 5 4 3 2 1

British Library Cataloguing in Publication Data

Horsley, Andy
    Skateboarding. – (Radical sports)
    1. Skateboarding – Juvenile literature
    I. Title
    769.2'2

Acknowledgements

The Publishers would like to thank Andy Horsley for permission to reproduce all photographs except p8–9 Tudor
Photography, p11a David Walker and p11b KPT Power Photos.

Cover photograph reproduced with permission of Andy Horsley.

Our thanks to Jane Bingham for her help in the preparation of this book. Thanks also to Kingham Hill School.

Every effort has been made to contact copyright holders of any material reproduced in this book. Any omissions will be
rectified in subsequent printings if notice is given to the Publisher.

This book aims to cover all the essential techniques of this radical sport but it is
important when learning a new sport to get expert tuition and to follow any
manufacturers' instructions.

CONTENTS

A short history of skateboarding

Skateboarding began in the late 1950s on the West Coast of America, where a group of bored Californian surfers tried putting a surfboard on rollerskate wheels.

The earliest skateboards were very crude and dangerous forms of transport. The main problem was their rattling steel wheels, which made the skateboard shake. The steel wheels were soon replaced by ones made of baked clay, and eventually in the early 1970s, by the smooth **urethane** plastic that is still used today.

A 1970s skateboarder prepares to kickturn.

The board shape stayed similar to the miniature wooden surfboard that it was modelled on. These 'old school' boards were made from wood, plastic or even metal and were designed to be cruised on. The introduction of the kicktail (an upturned back end) in the late 1960s allowed new tricks to be invented. There were many changes in board shape throughout the 1970s and '80s. Most modern boards are made from maple wood and have both a kicktail and an upturned nose.

Types of skateboarding

The two main types of skateboarding are street and ramp. Street skating is skateboarding using urban obstacles such as kerbs, stairs and **handrails**. This can be dangerous and is banned in some cities. However, many skateparks have streetcourses that copy the urban landscape. Skateparks offer a safe place to practise and can introduce you to ramp skating. These are also known as **halfpipes**, and are shaped like a letter 'U'. Ramps come in three main sizes – mini, midi and **vert**, which is vertical at the top.

Why skateboard?

Once you've stepped on a skateboard you'll understand why so many people love it. It holds many challenges and is constantly fun and exciting. As you begin to perfect tricks you will become more and more addicted to this fun pastime.

A massive air is held high above a vert ramp.

THE SKATEBOARD

Boards come in various sizes and widths, to suit different needs. There are several different types ranging from budget boards for beginners, which are sold in most high street sports shops, to professional boards, which are available in specialist skate shops.

Cheaper budget boards

As a beginner you will only need a cheap skateboard in order to become accustomed to its movement and basic manoeuvres. These boards are made from plywood rather than Canadian maple wood and the wheels tend to be low quality plastic. The feeling that you get when riding won't be smooth and flowing, but it's the easiest and cheapest way to see if skateboarding is for you.

Truckbolts

Four truckbolts are tightened through the deck and into each truck. These should be tight at all times to ensure stability and a solid ride.

Bearings

Bearings help the wheels to turn smoothly.

Griptape

This is a non-slip covering similar to sandpaper. This is on all skateboards and ensures that your feet stay exactly where you put them.

Professional standard boards

When you've decided to take skateboarding further you will need a professional standard skateboard, also known as a 'set-up'. Professional boards are so-called because the actual deck will usually bear the name of a world-class skateboarder; this will be his pro signature model. All the parts of a pro skateboard are sold separately and can be assembled by a skate shop assistant to create a professional set-up.

TOP TIP

If you've been introduced to skateboarding by a friend or relative, it would be worth asking if they or someone that they know has a second-hand skateboard. Always ask an experienced skateboarder to check the board out for you.

Tail

The back of the skateboard is called the kicktail and is also upturned to give leverage.

Wheel

The wheels will be **urethane** that will guarantee a smooth fast ride. Each wheel has two spaces for bearings, one in each side.

Nose

The front of the skateboard is called the nose and is slightly upturned.

Deck

The deck will be made from seven layers of quality maple wood glued and pressed together, with a high gloss finish and quality graphics.

Trucks

Each truck consists of two parts, baseplates which attach to the board and the hanger which the wheels bolt onto.

CLOTHES AND EQUIPMENT

As in all sports you need to protect yourself from falls. Skateboarding has some specialist equipment that has been designed with your safety in mind. As well as making sure that you have the necessary protective pads, you should wear heavy clothing such as jeans and a long sleeved top; loose baggy clothing will help you move easier and be less restrictive.

Elbow pads

When taking a fall it's often best to try to roll out of the fall, in a ball-like shape protecting all of your dangly bits, such as arms and legs. Elbow pads help you take a rolling fall by protecting your elbows.

Knee pads

If you tumble off your board while skating you are likely to fall on your knees. These plastic-capped friends are going to save your skin as well as your jeans.

Helmet

This is the most important piece of safety equipment. Made from hard plastic with a soft layer inside, the modern skate helmet is both comfy and easy to wear. Unlike a bicycle helmet, it is designed to protect your head from multiple impacts. (Many helmets now come with company graphics printed onto them, so you can be the envy of your skate mates.)

Wrist pads

These are essential for skateboarding. The most natural thing that you do when falling over is put your arms out to save yourself. Wrist pads have sections of plastic that protect your wrists and save your palms from road rash.

Skate shoes

There are lots of different makes of sports shoes that are designed specifically for skateboarding. These shoes are made of tougher materials than normal sports shoes. They will last a lot longer because they have tougher stitching and stronger soles.

Backpack

Carry a backpack with some choice skateboard survival equipment. Before you go anywhere make sure that you pack a bottle of water to stop you from dehydrating. A good skatetool is also an essential item to bring in your backpack – if anything comes loose or falls off, you could be in for a long walk home otherwise. A block of wax will help some stubborn obstacles grind. Also pack a box of plasters and some antiseptic cream in case you fall.

KEEPING FIT AND HEALTHY

Before you start skateboarding it's important to get the blood flowing around your body and warm up the appropriate muscles ready for action.

Warming up

Skateboarding uses a lot of leg action, so a few leg stretches and some knee bending will be the best place to start. This will help move the blood to your knees, ankles and thighs.

Body and arm stretches

These stretches will loosen up the rest of your body. Make sure that you keep your legs wide apart and as straight as you can. Touch the ground in front of you and then touch the toes on your right foot about ten times and then repeat on the left foot.

Rotation of ankles

Skateboarding puts an enormous strain on your ankles, so before venturing out, do 50 or so ankle rotations. Help your ankle to move by gently using your hands to spin and twist the foot (as if you were trying to take your feet off for the night). This will help your **ligaments** loosen up and reduce the chance of spraining, which will stop any fun that you are about to have!

Cooling down

To avoid your muscles becoming tight after skating you must cool down; simply jog on the spot or go for a brisk walk. This will ensure that you don't damage muscles or ligaments.

Nutrition

If you want to skate all day, the best way to keep your energy levels up is by eating the right food. The main source of energy comes from carbohydrate-rich food such as pasta, potatoes and bread. Drink plenty of water throughout the day to replenish your fluids and maybe carry a few energy bars in your backpack.

Running helps you maintain fitness.

Eating plenty of fresh vegetables helps to keep you healthy.

WHERE TO SKATE

There are many different skateboard parks for you to visit, each containing different obstacles.

Concrete

Concrete parks were popular in the 1960s and '70s and are now making a comeback. Concrete parks are like a smooth lunar landscape with dips and **bowls** to roll around on. Concrete is very smooth but also very fast, so take care out there.

An outdoor concrete park.

Wooden parks

Wooden parks are nearly always indoors. You may well have to pay a small fee to skate inside a park, but the money goes towards the upkeep of the obstacles. The obstacles that you may find will include **halfpipes** and mini-ramps (which are small halfpipes), flat wooden banks, **quarterpipes**, **grind boxes** and metal **handrails** that simulate outdoor handrails. Most of the obstacles are built to simulate a real street environment.

You may well enter your first competition in one of these indoor parks, so it's good to get the feel of a few different ones if you can. Check with the owner and find out if any teams will be visiting to do demos or displays.

Outdoor skate ramps

Outdoor ramps are either metal or wood halfpipes ranging from mini-ramp to **vert**-ramp. These are only skateable during good weather and it is dangerous to skate them at any other time.

Street skating

Sometimes you may want to practise in a local park or an empty street, but street skating can be very dangerous. It is now illegal to skate on some streets, so if you see the 'no skateboarding' signs it's best to find somewhere else. When you go out to skate around the streets make sure that you travel with a few friends, so that if you **slam** or something happens, you'll be in good hands.

An indoor wooden park.

SAFETY FIRST

- Be aware of other skaters.
- Look out for wet surfaces.
- Always wear full protective skate pads.
- Be aware of your speed and direction.

THE BASICS

Are you goofy?

There are two different ways of standing on a skateboard. You're either **goofy** (right foot forward) or **regular** (left foot forward). You will have to experiment in order to find out which is your riding **stance**. Try sliding across the kitchen floor in socks; whichever foot leads your slide will be the leading foot on the board. Or stand on your board in each stance, lean left and right and move around on the spot until you feel comfortable one way or the other.

Goofy and regular skateboarders battle it out on a mini-ramp.

Moving off

After finding the most comfortable stance you will want to make your board move! Place your leading foot at the front of the board over the truck bolts – if your feet cover these bolts your balance should be perfect. Use your back foot as a paddle to push the board along. When you and the board are moving, place the back foot over the back bolts. While you are moving, bend your knees and use your arms to help you balance. Stay over the board until the board comes to a standstill.

The tic-tac

The tic-tac will keep you moving after you've pushed off. With a tic-tac you lift the front wheels slightly off the ground and move the board to the left and to the right. This creates a sidewinder motion like a snake, which in turn propels you forward.

Dropping off

When **dropping off** things like small ledges or kerbs, hold your feet over the truck bolts and keep your body weight and balance equal over the front and the back. Ride off the object keeping the board level by adjusting your balance. After the rear wheels have cleared the ledge the board will touchdown onto the floor. Make sure all four wheels hit the ground at the same time and bend your knees to absorb the impact.

SLOWING, STOPPING AND FALLING

Slowing down

If you feel you're moving too fast and you want to slow yourself down, simply take your back foot off the board and use the sole as a brake, applying the flat of your shoe to the ground. You can also use this as a means of stopping. Another way to slow down is to lean back and use your back foot to press the tail down onto the floor, but you need to be more confident for this one and it does wear out your board.

Stopping

The most obvious way to stop moving is to simply step off to the side and pick up your board. This will be all right while you're learning, but as you gain confidence you can explore more stylish ways to stop, including the most commonly used 'step off and **grab**'. This involves taking the front foot off the board, placing it on the floor to the **heelside** and propping the board up with the back foot, allowing you to pick the skateboard up holding the nose.

Falling safely

There could be a moment where you may not be able to
stop in time, so you need to know how to fall safely.

The roll method

1. When you feel you are about to fall
off (**bailing**), step off the side of your
board and perform a relaxed roll.

2. Make yourself into a ball, being careful
not to leave your hands and wrists
sticking out.

3. It's human nature to put your hands down
first, but try to land on your side rolling away
from the board.

The knee slide

When bailing on ramps
your knee pads will save you.
Before you start **slamming**
(a hard, uncontrolled fall),
fall to your knees keeping
them together and **slide**
down the ramp **transition**
on your knees.

MORE TECHNIQUES

180 degrees slide to fakie

Add a little spice by sliding the board around 180° to go backwards known as riding **fakie**!

As you're riding forward with your feet over the truck bolts, release some weight off your back foot and use it to push the back of the board around 180° – the front foot will act as a pivot.

Make sure that your body follows the board around until the whole board and yourself are travelling backwards.

Skating transitions

Skating ramps is often called skating **transitions**. Start at the top of the ramp with the tail of the skateboard held onto the **lip** with your back foot and the front of the skateboard sticking out over the ramp. Place your front foot over the front trucks and push off. Aim to apply all four wheels to the ramp surface as soon as you can. Lean forwards but stay over the board and ride down the ramp.

Once you've dropped in you'll soon reach the other side. In order to keep your speed you have to work the transitions; this is called pumping. As you ride up the transition thrust your body forwards and upwards towards the lip; as you roll back down the transition thrust downwards and roll fast across the flat bottom of the ramp.

Turning (carving)

After you have practised this for a while you can start to learn turning, or **carving**. Apply weight and pressure to either the **toeside** or the **heelside** of the board. If you lean toeside you will make the board turn inwards (**backside**). Leaning heelside will turn the board outwards (**frontside**).

Kickturning

Kickturns are needed to turn around on a ramp. Backside kickturns are often the easiest to do.

1. Roll up the transition.

2 + 3. When you are close to the top of the ramp (the lip) lift the front wheels slightly and carve your body and board around to face back down the transition.

4. Place all four wheels back down and ride down the ramp.

THE OLLIE

The Ollie is the basis for nearly all the skateboard tricks that you can think of. This trick has been around since the late 1970s and was invented by a skateboarder named Alan 'Ollie' Gelfand. The Ollie is basically a jump, but this trick is very important. It will have you pulling your hair out, but if you stick with it, it'll give you years of pleasure.

This is where the curved ends of your skateboard come into play – the spade shaped 'tail' of your skateboard is the key to the Ollie. The key to a good Ollie is all in the timing, so practice is a must with this stunt. Start learning this trick moving very slowly. This trick requires that you move your back foot away from the safety of your truck bolts and rest the toes in the centre of the tail; your front foot can stay over the front truck bolts.

A good example of an Ollie grab!

The trick consists of seven steps:

1. As you ride along with your back foot toes in the centre of the tail, bend your knees as if to power up your legs for a big jump.
2. Using your back foot, hit the tail down hard on the ground (in order to do this you must take weight off the front foot). The board will tip up backwards.

3. As the tail hits the ground you must jump upwards sliding your front foot along the griptape towards the end of the nose.
4. This scraping will pull the board upwards. Your back foot should leave the board allowing the back end of the skateboard to take off as well.
5. You will have jumped taking your board with you. Level out your feet and skateboard and prepare to return to the ground.
6. As you touchdown, your feet should be back over the truck bolts for perfect stability and balance.
7. Ride away with a smile on your face.

You'll always remember where and when you first learnt to Ollie.

The Ollie is **THE** trick to learn if you want to take skateboarding any further than just moving, but it does take time and patience to learn.

Now that you understand the Ollie here are a few tricks that involve it.

Grinds

The section of your truck in between the wheels is the **grinding** area. Grinds are when your trucks come into contact with a surface and you travel on the trucks instead of the wheels. Grinds can be on kerbs, ramp **coping**, **grind boxes** or **handrails**.

Basic 50-50 grind

A 50-50 grind is where you Ollie onto an object and grind both trucks along the obstacle. The thing to remember about grinds is to go quite fast and keep your weight over the trucks.

Boardslides

Boardslides are **sliding** along a block, rail or ramp coping using the belly of the board to slide. No contact is made by the wheels. Travel toes forward, balancing on the board's middle. This takes a lot of practice and a lot of balance, but feels good when you've mastered it.

Balance and skill are needed to perform a long 50-50 such as this.

Nose and tailslides

Noseslides are achieved by ollieing up onto the nose and sliding along an obstacle using the nose as the sliding area. This involves pressure being applied to the nose which helps it slide along the obstacle.

A night-time backside tailslide comes to an end.

The tailslide is pretty much the same but instead of using the front end of the board to slide you use the tail, applying pressure and forward momentum to help the tail slide.

Wheelies

This is a simple trick that will help you perfect your balance. The nose of the board is held up above the ground while the back wheels are travelling along. You can Ollie up onto platforms landing in wheelie position and try to ride along balanced on the back wheels for as long as you can.

Kickflips

The kickflip is what most skaters want to learn first but this move definitely comes after the Ollie. A kickflip involves the board being kicked with the front foot allowing the board to flip around its length. It spins around 360° and lands back with all four wheels down. Many hours will be used learning this trick and even with years of practice it will still be difficult to pull off.

Your skateboard should be looked after to ensure a perfect and safe ride every time. Here are a few things that you should regularly check or change.

Wheels

Wheels tend to cone outwards after a while which means that they wear down on the outer edge. This can be solved by turning the wheels around and skating them back to normal.

Bearings

Bearings can become rusted and squeaky, especially if you have ridden through water. Some bearings can be dismantled and cleaned; this is a tricky job but can sometimes work very well. Bearings should be cleaned with a spray lubricant (oil) and then greased. Sometimes the actual ball bearings have been damaged which means replacing them with new bearings.

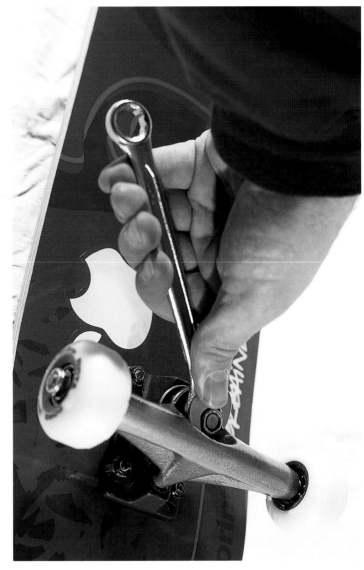

Make sure wheels are tight at all times – you don't want them falling off!

Truck bushings

Truck bushings are the two rubber blocks that live between the hanger and the baseplate. They do split after a while but are very cheap and can bring old worn-out trucks back to life.

Trucks

Trucks will last you a long time and, in some cases, even years. Sometimes baseplates snap but you can buy these separately.

Kingpin

The kingpin is the bolt that holds the hanger of the truck onto the baseplate and can snap if stressed. These are cheap but you'll have to take the whole truck off to change it.

Griptape

Griptape can sometimes become blocked with dirt and lose its grip. Dab the griptape with a wet sponge, and then soak the water off with kitchen towel. You can also replace damaged griptape.

You can buy various skate tools that will contain all of the right size sockets and screwdriver heads. Some are small and quite technical, and some come with a few different tools. The best ones usually come with everything attached, so you won't lose the different parts.

A typical skate tool.

TOP TIP

Try to look after your board and make sure that you don't take it out in wet weather. It's bad news for your deck and could also be dangerous. Leave the water to the surfers!

TAKING IT FURTHER

All around the world there are skateboard competitions and events being held almost every weekend. These events allow spectators to see some amazing skate stars going crazy and young up-and-coming amateur skaters to be seen. These events are usually advertised in skateboard magazines and in your local skate shops. They are loads of fun and offer a chance both to see your heroes in action and maybe have a go yourself.

There are two main categories in a skateboard competition – **vert** ramp riding and street style.

Vert ramp riding

Vert riding is another name for skating a vertical skateboard ramp. This is very spectacular and is often the way that skateboarding is first encountered. The vert competition usually consists of 45-second runs for each rider to do as many tricks as he or she can without falling off. They are then judged by the technical difficulty of their runs. Sometimes there is a 'highest air' section in the vert competition. This is a real crowd-pleaser and has skaters trying to jump as high as they can out of the top of the ramp and then land back in again.

Competition-standard vert ramp riding in action.

Street style

A huge section of the arena where the skate competition is held will be devoted to replicating obstacles and objects that you would find in a real street environment. The street area is where you will see the most death-defying tricks being tried and fierce trick combinations attempted. At the end of a good street competition there will be a 'best trick' prize.

Sponsorship

Becoming sponsored will mean getting free skateboard gear, and possibly even being paid to skateboard – but sponsorship should never be chased. As you become more and more confident at skating you may enter some competitions and achieve a high placing. This is a good way of being seen and getting your name around the skate circuit. Always remember there will be many other budding skaters out there hoping for the same thing. It's best to let the sponsorship come to you if you're lucky and talented enough. The best way to have fun is to just skateboard for yourself.

Boardsliding at an indoor skate park.

SKATING STARS

Skateboarders can now be found in any country and this provides for a wealth of talent. Often skaters travel around the globe in structured teams doing demonstrations and entering competitions. Here are some names that you may even recognise.

Tony Hawk

Without a doubt the most famous skateboarder alive (he even has his own computer game), Tony was the first person to land a 900 – that's two and a half full spins out of the top of the ramp. He has also completed the loop the loop, skateboarding upside down around a fullpipe (a full circle of wood, concrete or metal that can be skated using frontside and backside carves).

Bob Burnquist

Bob grew up skating very poorly maintained concrete skateparks in Brazil and he is now one of the world's most talented vert ramp riders. Bob is known for his switchstance skating abilities (to ride the opposite way to your normal stance).

Tony Hawk is so good on a **vert** ramp that they have now started to build special ramps just for him to skate, with massive gaps to jump and other death-defying obstacles included.

Eric Koston

Eric was born in Thailand but moved to California when he was young. Often hailed as the 'god' of street skating, Eric has the ability to string together very technical tricks. He has also made sponsorship money by promoting a top-selling shoe design.

Elissa Steamer

Elissa Steamer has been skateboarding since she was twelve and turned professional in 1998. Since then she has risen through the ranks of professional skateboarding to stand amongst some of the best skateboarders in the world.

Tom Penny

Tom grew up skateboarding the streets of Oxford in England. When he moved to the USA everyone noticed how relaxed and confident he was. At every competition Tom would cruise around and make difficult tricks look simple. Tom can also skate vert with the same ease and precision, which makes him one of the most rounded skateboarders alive today.

The world record for the highest Ollie on flat ground was won by Danny Wainwright, a professional skateboarder from Bristol, England who popped an Ollie 109 centimetres (44.5 inches) over a barrier.

Tom Penny

GLOSSARY

backside   a turn or move with your back facing outwards and your toes facing inwards

bailing   the act of leaving your skateboard before you crash. Not to be confused with slamming.

bowl   a concrete skatepark obstacle that resembles a huge breakfast bowl. Usually made from smooth, fast concrete. Sometimes wooden bowls are made for indoor parks.

carve   to turn the board at speed without sliding on the wheels, usually on a ramp or bank

coping   the top edge or lip of a ramp, bowl or block. On ramps this is made from metal tubing.

drop off   to ride off something involving a drop, such as a kerb or block

fakie   riding backwards

frontside   a turn with your chest facing outwards and heels facing inwards

goofy   standing with your right foot on the front of the skateboard, pushing with your left foot

grab   where you grab the board during a trick

grind   riding along the truck's surface rather than the wheels

grind box   a box or block with an edge or coping that you can grind along

halfpipe   a big 'U'-shaped tube with a flat bottom, usually made from wood but sometimes concrete or metal

handrails   metal handrails that go down stairs

heelside   the side of the board closest to the inside of your heel (right for goofy stance, left for regular)

ligaments   tough bands of elastic tissue that hold joints together

lip   the 90° angle that identifies the top edge of a ramp or bowl

quarterpipe   half of a halfpipe; one transition or one curve

regular   standing with your left foot on the front of the skateboard, pushing with your right foot

slamming   a hard uncontrolled or unexpected fall

slide   to slide on parts of the deck; to slide on the knees to avoid injury

stance   the position you stand on a board, either goofy or regular

toeside   the side of the board closest to your toe (left for goofy stance, right for regular)

transition   the curve or bend of a ramp

urethane   a high-quality plastic used for making wheels

vert   jump ramp which has a vertical section at the top

FURTHER READING

Books

Extreme Sports: Skateboarding, Ben Powell,
Franklin Watts, 1997

Skateboard Roadmap, James Davis,
Carlton Books, 2000

To the Limit: Skateboarding, Andy Horsley,
Hodder Wayland Publishers, 2001

Thrasher: Insane Terrain,
Universe Publishing, 2001

Hawk: Occupation: Skateboarder,
Tony Hawk & Sean Mortimer (contributor)
Regan Books, 2001

Super.activ: Skateboarding, James Marsh,
Hodder Children's Books, 2000

Magazines

Sidewalk skate mag,
Permanent Publishing

Transworld Skateboarding,
Warner Publishing

Thrasher magazine,
High Speed Productions

Websites

www.skateboard.com
Everything you need to know about
skateboarding

www.network26.com
Home site of Sidewalk UK skate magazine

www.skateboardermag.com
Home of skateboarder magazine

www.skateboarding.com
Home of Transworld skate magazine

www.ukskatenews.com
News from the UK skate scene

INDEX

Titles in the *Radical Sports* series include:

Hardback   0 431 03695 0

Hardback   0 431 03690 X

Hardback   0 431 03692 6

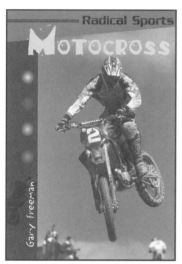

Hardback   0 431 03691 8

Hardback   0 431 03694 2

Hardback   0 431 03693 4

Find out about the other titles in this series on our website www.heinemann.co.uk/library